T0123359

IS IT ME,
IS IT MY HAIR,
IS IT MY SKIN COLOR,
IS IT MY EYES,
OR IS IT YOU?

*The Real Relationship Between African American
Women and White American Women*

BRENDA Y. PERSON, Ph.D. & JANE K. FIELDINGS, BGS

authorHOUSE®

AuthorHouse™
1663 Liberty Drive
Bloomington, IN 47403
www.authorhouse.com
Phone: 1 (800) 839-8640

Published by AuthorHouse 03/29/2019

ISBN: 978-1-5462-7243-4 (sc)
ISBN: 978-1-5462-7245-8 (e)

Library of Congress Control Number: 2019903201

Print information available on the last page.

IS IT ME,
IS IT MY HAIR,
IS IT MY SKIN COLOR,
IS IT MY EYES,
OR IS IT YOU?

**OUR PERCEPTION OF RELATIONSHIP
BETWEEN AFRICAN AMERICAN WOMEN
AND WHITE AMERICAN WOMEN**

CONTENTS

DEDICATION

This book is dedicated to our children, grandchildren and future great-grandchildren

Brenda's Children
Jibri K. Person
Asha Shani Person, Deceased

Brenda's Grandchild
Gregory Logan Person

Jane's Children
Nichole Green
Jeremy Jones

Jane's Grandchildren
Acealeyah Dothard
Amos Dothard, Deceased

We MARCH, y'all mad.
We SIT DOWN y'all mad.
We SPEAK UP, y'all mad.
We DIE, y'all silent.

The most disrespected person in
America is the Black Woman
-Malcolm X

The short question is why don't we like each other? The short answer is: we are better than you, but the long answer is: well it is not that we don't like you or think that we are better than you. There are societal complications that interfere with a wholesome relationship. We have too much history that places invisible barriers to real relationships based on questions that are not asked or answered. What have we said? Nothing. Behind a simple question there are always multiple questions that are assumed but never asked. Positive relationships are built on those hidden questions that are not asked but one is able to bring them to the forefront whether they are asked or not. African American women and white American women need to step outside of the box to communicate. Do they really want to know each other; probably not? Why? A great relationship needs to be beneficial to both participants. We don't want to share. What is mine is mine and what is yours is also mine. After all, I am the privileged one, I deserve it. We value the message but not the messenger. It is alright to have big hips, but we don't like yours. We have not developed a culture of reciprocal appreciation.

Our relationship is based on personal results of making

each other feel devalued and misused. Our relationship is based on how we treat you so that you will remain in your own space and not intrude into our space which we both think that we own. Our relationship misses the most important prerequisite for relationships; the five-letter word trust, and the seven-letter word, respect. If one lives to be seventy years old and is considered to be an average person, he or she will spend twenty years sleeping, twenty years working, six years eating, seven years playing, five years dressing, one year on the phone, two and a half years smoking, two and a half years in bed, three years waiting for someone, five months tying shoes and two and a half years for other things. How much time is spent on building positive relationships between African American women and white American women? A real true relationship takes more time and effort than most of us do not have or care to have.

We see the fear on your face when a racial issue comes up in conversation. We see padded conversations around interracial marriages; don't say anything because it may offend the white sister in-law, girl friend or daughter in-law.

African American big lips were ugly but white American women's puffed lips are beautiful. African American women's big butts were unattractive until white American women's big butts became sexy. Now all big butts are sexy. It is alright to have big butts, but we don't like your big butt. It is alright to have big lips, but we don't like your big lips. Our big butts come with a history. It is said that some nomad African women had big butts during harvest time because they stored fat that allowed them to survive during the lean season. We are more than big butts; we are survivors. We have a history. Who are African American women really and why is there no bond with white American women? Where did the mistrust begin and why has it persisted over the centuries?

Sisterhood is not about race.
Sisterhood is about connection.

CHAPTER 1

WHERE IT ALL BEGAN, SLAVERY

My father used to say that stories are part of
the most precious heritage of mankind.
-Tahiu Shah

Cultural Norms

In the South before the Civil War, many slaves were diagnosed with forms of mental illness because their behavior violated cultural norms. Drapetomania was a psychological disorder in which a slave had an uncontrollable urge to escape from bondage. Dysaesthesia Aethiopica was a disorder in which a slave was disobedient to her or his owners. Although labeling the desire to be free and the resentment of human bondage as disorders seems ludicrous today, such labeling illustrates how culture can shape our perception of mental illness. How many false perceptions of truth prevail today?

Albert Einstein is thought to have said, "I think the most important question facing humanity is, is the universe a friendly place?" It is up to us to decide whether to believe in a friendly or hostile world. When you trust in goodness, that is what you tend to find. If no one will step up and admit that we have some responsibility for the pain of others, there is an impasse with communication and a denial that our behavior will have an impact beyond our current time in history.

Slavery was so long ago. Can't you forget about it? Our answer is, no. Our lives are like an open book that forms a real life's narrative. Whether one thinks it is worth reading depends on their willingness to form an authentic relationship. It is much easier to show your own photos than for you to look at my book. The United States was not a nation until 1776; therefore, we cannot be accountable for the years of slavery before the country was founded; therefore, Blacks were not in slavery for four hundred years. You cannot claim that you were in slavery for four hundred years because there was no nation. Makes sense, doesn't it? Maybe to you but not to the discordances of slavery.

Our lives have a way of accelerating, making the past not so distant. Count it by hours, count it by days, count it by years and however you count it, it will add up to a life time of repercussions from slavery. Every aspect of African American women's lives is influenced by the aftermath of slavery including health care, economics, education, housing, religion and entertainment. Nothing can undo history and we cannot let history repeat itself. Reversal is not a choice. So, we dig our heels in and try to build a relationship with you. Who will step across the line first? There is a system set in place to deliberately inhibit our chances to succeed. To understand African American women, you cannot ignore our history, as ugly as it may be. It is what we bring to the table. I found it odd and amusing that a person of another race would recommend that I go see "I am not your Negro" by James Baldwin because I would find it insightful and an eye opener. Really? "The objective reality is that virtually no one who is white understands the challenge of being black in America." Pin a sign on the back of a white American woman that says treat me like I am black and pin a sign on the back of an African American woman that says treat me like I am white. What do you think would happen?

In a foreword to the book, Post Traumatic Slave Syndrome authored by Joy DeGruy Ph.D., Randall Robinson writes that African Americans are being urged to forget slavery, to forget Jim Crow and to forget about what Africa was prior to the advent of trans-Atlantic slavery. "In as much as African Americans are the only Americans whose forebears were dragooned to America against their will and enslaved in American for nearly three centuries, a curiosity about our past, questions about ancestors known and unknown, and a need to know about Africa before we were torn from its breast is not only normal, but, indeed, is a sign of a healthy intellect, psyche, and a soul." What is so bad about the middle passage, slavery, Jim Crow, lynching, killings by policemen, unemployment, uneducated, undereducated, poverty, drug infested neighborhoods, violence? Get over it; move on!

Let us be realistic; we didn't get off to a happy beginning. We started as slaves. There was no sisterhood bonding. It must be remembered that it was not just men who owned the enslaved. Some women built up their own plantations and others inherited estates from deceased husbands. Enslaved women were often given to white women as gifts from their husbands and as wedding and Christmas gifts or if young as companions or play friends. Harriet Jacobs in *Incidents of a Slave Girl* (1861) was scathing about the treatment meted out by the slave owner's wives explaining it as retaliation for their husband's sexual interaction with enslaved women. The mistress, who ought to protect the helpless victim, has no other feelings towards her but those of jealousy and rage. Mary Prince recorded that Mrs. Flint's nerves were so strong, that she could sit in her easy chair and see a woman whipped, till the blood trickled from every stroke of the lash. If dinner was not served at the exact time on that Sunday, she would station herself in the kitchen, and wait till it was dished, and then spit in all the kettles and pans that had been used. Perhaps she thought this would prevent the slaves from eating left overs.

In the past, it was assumed that female slave owners

were not as brutal as their male counterparts. However, there was no a sex divide. There were good and bad male and female slave owners. Some of the harshest treatments could be meted out by a slave owner's wife against a female slave who her husband had been intimate with or an enslaved child that was the result of a sexual encounter between her husband and a slave. Some European women took out revenge on the enslaved for their punishment by cruel fathers or husbands. European women's cruelty shocked many observers in the Caribbean. Mary Prince stated that her mistress caused me to know the exact difference between the smart of the rope, the cart-whip, and the cow-skin, when applied to my naked body by her own cruel hand. And there was scarcely any punishment more dreadful than the blows I received on my face and head from her hard, heavy fist. She was a fearful woman, and a savage mistress to her slaves. White women must have been angry at black slave women because their husbands considered sexual access to them as part of his property rights. Are they still angry? Enslaved women usually had a double task as a slave and as a wife and mother. As a result, women often worked much harder than men. The physical abuse bestowed on the enslaved persons was generally not gender separated. Whether a man or a woman, a slave received equal amounts of physical abuse such as beatings.

While some historians, such as C. Vann Woodward and Catherine Clinton, have argued that white women were secretly opposed to the system of slavery, scholar Elizabeth Fox-Genovese demolished this notion with her work, Within the Plantation Household: Black and White Women in the Old South Fox-Genovese draws on white slaveholding women's diaries, letters, and postbellum memoirs, along with the Works Progress Administration's narratives of enslaved black women as her source of material to make a convincing argument that even though they worked in the same households there was no "shared sense of sisterhood" among black and white women.

Why is there a lack of relationship and bonding among white American women and African American women? The disconnect comes when one party fails to acknowledge the present lasting influence of slavery. Can't we all just get along? Slavery happened a long time ago so why can't you get over it? These refrains about a distant, non-slaveholding past are commonplace among white people. The first is meant to suggest a lack of connection to the institution of slavery, and therefore, a lack of responsibility for understanding it; and the second is meant to suggest that historical amnesia is a salve for social ills. Just as slavery could not have been successful without the help of white American women, neither could discrimination and Jim Crow laws.

It must be remembered that it was not just men who owned the enslaved. Some women built up their own plantations and others inherited estates from deceased husbands. Also, some wives were given enslaved workers by their husbands as gifts, or by fathers to daughters mainly to carry out the household chores, or were if young as companions or play friends, like Mary Prince was in her early days in slavery. Other wives brought slaves to carry out their own small ventures, with a bit of independence from their husbands. Harriet Jacobs wrote in Incidents in the Life of a Slave Girl that sexual relations between elite white women and enslaved men, "how upper-class white women who engaged in these (relationships with male slaves) relationships used sex as an instrument of power, simultaneously perpetuating both white supremacy and patriarchy."

Why? "Some of them were simply bored or sexually frustrated. But perhaps, at least on a subconscious level, sexual exploitation of slaves was a means of compensating for their lack of power in other aspects of their lives."

Given the context of white women during this period in history, this is a plausible reason for sexual relations with slaves. It would also address the failure of white women to "defend" or attempt to prevent the mistreatment of slaves. The women slaves were looked upon as competition, or even as an object of jealousy whereas the black male slave's true affections were with the black slave woman. Sexual relations with black male slaves gave white women a feeling of power, supremacy, superiority over the black woman.

A culture which held white women in the highest esteem would not enable a white woman to stand against the system. That supremacy enabled the slavery system to remain but specifically placed her above her "sisters", women of color who were enslaved. Black women sexual rivals?
White male dominance must surely have damaged the white female psyche. Attention white slave masters aimed at black female slaves surely provoked resentment among slave master's white female mates and this attention did not gone unnoticed. Society held that black women were inherently lustful, possibly creating fantasies in the white masters in contrast to the pureness of the white female.

Harriet Jacobs was able to write well because her mistress until age 12, was considered a kind, considerate friend, (in her opinion) who taught her to read and spell. In addition, Harriet was placed in circumstances with intellectual persons who gave her opportunities for self-improvement.

No matter how kind, white female slave owners did not set slaves free when they had the power to do so. Upon the death of the mistress, the black female slave was bequeathed (as chattel) to another family member. The mistress did not own many slaves but each one was either bequeathed to family or put on the auction block. Either way the slave was gotten rid of but not freed.

The mistress taught "Whatsoever ye would that men should do unto you, do ye even unto them." "Thou shalt love they neighbor as thyself." Apparently, the mistress did not recognize her slave as her neighbor. A young girl's slave mistress borrowed money from the slave woman and promised to pay it back without benefit of a written promise to repay. This is the "good friend" whom the slave woman trusted. The money was not paid back.

Sophia Auld had never owned a slave before Fredrick Douglass. She became Douglass's slave mistress. "She was the pinnacle of white womanhood; caring, benevolent, a woman of the kindest heart and finest feelings." Slave ownership turned her into a monster. In his 1845 Narrative of the Life of Fredrick Douglass, Douglass describes her transformation from a kind woman who tried to help him learn how to write, into a cruel mistress. The Narrative of the Life of Frederick Douglass Quotes says, "The fatal poison of irresponsible power was already in her hands and soon commenced its infernal work." Accounts of slavery and white women vary. Sometimes a white woman starts out kind and becomes cruel; sometimes cruel becoming seemingly kinder.

Mammy took care of the white children and the white family took care of Mammy. Mammy is characterized by whites as an asexual woman. (Mammy was maternal and deeply religious). Mammy type women worked in the house and wore better clothes than the field slaves. This was not better treatment of the Mammy slave. This better treatment reflected of the owner's wealth.

Enslaved women were accused of being seductresses, a "Jezebel", tempting the white master. Even now, black women are portrayed as oversexualized or "Jezebels" by the media. Images of the Mammy stereotype are still prevalent as well as in Aunt Jemima. Mammy is viewed as a "safe" black woman which whites (women) are comfortable with. Mistresses often beat enslaved women for having sex with their husbands. The husband was not held accountable.

Madame LaLaurie, a New Orleans socialite, owned a mansion in New Orleans circa 1833. She owned slaves. A slave girl, Leah, accidentally snagged Madame LaLaurie's hair as she combed it. Madame LaLaurie chased Leah around the room with a whip. The girl ran down a hallway that led to a balcony. Holding on to the railing to escape the whip, Leah's foot slipped, and she fell to her death. Madame LaLaurie was charged a $300 fine for abusing slaves. Her mistreated slaves were taken from her and sold at auction. Madame LaLaurie sent a relative to purchase the slaves and return them to her. Slave quarters were attached to Madame's mansion. The quarters were in deplorable condition and the slaves appeared to be starved.

A fire occurred at Madame's mansion in 1834. Firemen

found disfigured bodies of slaves who had been locked in a small attic crawl space. The enslaved appeared to be victims of medical experiments and were chained to walls. One male slave appeared to have undergone a botched gender re-assignment surgery while a female slave had her arms amputated and skin pulled off. Two slaves were discovered chained to the kitchen stove. It is reported that the slaves were chained to the stove when they attempted to get food to the slaves. It is believed these two may have set the fire to alert the authorities of their plight. A contradictory report states that "a slave chained to the stove confessed to setting the fire as a form of suicide. Slaves were said to fear punishment going to the 'upper room' from whence no one ever returned." Some slaves were found suspended by their neck when firefighters went in. Slaves with limbs stretched and torn claimed to have been in that position for months. Slaves were found buried under floor boards during a renovation. Neighbors reported screams. Some were found hung or stretched by their limbs; others had missing body parts. Other slaves were found wearing spiked collars.

Madame LaLaurie was known to put mangled, tortured bodies on display. The crowds were so appalled that LaLaurie's mansion was overrun. The LaLaurie's family escaped to Paris to avoid prosecution. There are reports that Madame LaLaurie was polite to blacks and solicitous of her slave's health. There are court records of her freeing her slaves.

Coerced sex was used by white females to perpetuate white supremacy. White women took out their frustrations on enslaved males they owned with excessive violence, cruelty and forced sex to combat feelings of powerlessness in a patriarchal society. "Some (male slaves) are disobedient wrote a Southern mistress. Much idleness, sullenness, slovenliness . . . used the rod." Thavolia Glymph challenges the depiction of mistresses as "friends" or allies of slaves. Mistresses were powerful in the hierarchy of slavery. Glymph cites systematic violence by women against enslaved women and debunks the idea of some form of gender solidarity trumping race and class in slave households. Whatever was done has had a lasting impact on the relationship between African American women and white American women. It has prevailed and been passed down with our genes.

Alex Manly, editor of the Daily Record, published an editorial challenging the myth of pure white womanhood stating, "our experience among poor white people in the country teaches us that women of that race are not any more particular in the matter of clandestine meetings with colored men than the white men with colored women." Is the experience among poor whites any different than the experience among well-off whites? The main difference is financial.

White women cannot comprehend that they could be oppressed and still be oppressive. "White women will try to ravage us from the inside out with a smile, a comment, a betrayal, a vital inaction, a look." They "choose comfort over effort."

CHAPTER 2

RACISM

An old Chinese proverb says that the beginning of wisdom is to call all things by their proper names.

Race definition one is usually defined as the act or process of some type of competition or contest with the idea that there are winners and there are losers. How much of that is carried over to race definition two? Race definition two usually refers to some sort of classification system that tries to place humans into some type of groups defined by anatomical, culture, ethnic, genetic, geographical locations, or other social affiliations and even skin coloring. This brings back around the concept that there is some hierarchal favoritism and there must be a winner. We dress it up by using words like racial and ethnicity, but it is all the same. There will always be a winner and a loser.

There are thousands of ways to express how we feel about each other. Love is not one of them, but race is. Where is the love? Love is hidden behind race in the way we respond and react to each other. Race looks a lot like our actions. Speak one word and we know. James Baldwin said, "If you lie about me, then you will lie about yourself."

Southern eugenicists believed that if they strictly policed the race lines any hereditary defects of blacks would remain with them and not corrupt the white race. This blueprint was researched and put into extreme use by Hitler. Galton flatly asserted that whites were superior to the African Negro. In the deep south, Federated Women's Clubs, played a decisive role in stabilizing eugenically segregated institutions for the mentally retarded, partly based on Paul Popenoe's 1918 applied eugenics: The Negro race must be placed very near zero on the scale. Scientific racism was promoted by the University of VA. Leading the charge was Ivey Lewis Foreman and Robert Bennett Bean. Bean's paper is entitled "Some Racial Peculiarities of the Negro Brain".

President Warren G. Harding from Ohio was a supporter of eugenicist.

African American women seem to be able to read white American women racist body language because we encounter it so often. White American women seem to take a see nothing, hear nothing, speak nothing, do nothing attitude. The Penn State victims are ignored, and the mate lives off a hefty pension. Emmitt Till was lynched. The accuser lived happily ever after. More than 60 years after an all-white, all-male jury acquitted two Mississippi men in fourteen-year old Emmett Till's death, Carolyn Bryant Donhamm, the accuser, admitted she lied.

Emmett Till was beaten and murdered for allegedly whistling at Roy Bryant's wife, Carolyn. Till's body was found floating in the Tallahatchie River so badly swollen and disfigured he was unrecognizable. His mother requested an open casket to show the world what was done to her son. Presumably, Carolyn would have seen or at least heard about this.

Under oath, Carolyn Bryant testified that Emmett had grabbed and physically threatened her alleging that he told her he had *"done something"* with white women before. In 2007, Bryant admitted that she lied about that part of the story. She said the rest of what happened at the store that day is a blurred memory. She is now 84 years old. Her whereabouts have been kept secret by her family. Carolyn claims she felt grief and remorse after the murder claiming the case ruined her life. Ruined her life? At least she had a life. What about Emmett Till's family, specifically his mother? "Nothing that boy did could ever justify what happened to him," she said. Bryant expressed sorrow and sympathy for Till's mother and couldn't imagine her pain until losing one of her own sons. Carolyn Bryant claims she "thought" the old system of white supremacy was wrong though she took it (and took advantage of it) as normal at that time. In reading her account, notice the emphasis she places on herself. Her feelings are emphasized. She knew or should have known the outcome for Emmett Till when she told that lie. Notice how conveniently memories are blurred as to what really happened. This is, in our opinion, an example of how white women used and use their white supremacy to their advantage. Does that mean she committed some transgression for which she was covering up? A transgression so grievous she allowed an innocent person (child) to be put to death? Was she protecting her own interests?

CHAPTER 3

DISRESPECT

You should respect each other and refrain from disputes.
You should not, like water and oil, repel each other, but
should, like milk and water, mingle together. -Buddha

Everyone's life forms a narrative but if you never open the book you only see the cover. We are only a photo that you can interpret as you wish. Our losses, our gains, our hopes, our dreams are never acknowledged. As well as we can read you, we were shocked at your position on the pedestal when you supported a political party and presidential candidate that insulted you and sees you as merely a vile sex object. We shake our heads as you flock to foreign countries, spend thousands of dollars to adopt children when the social services in the United States have thousands of children who need homes and adoption of these children is free. It is appalling that you would say that it is about time that Americans realized that everyone cannot have a free education. We live from the inside out not outside in. What is going on inside will eventually be displayed as your true feelings on the outside. Our inner thoughts will always emerge and show who we really are. Inner thoughts identify the dis-joints in our relationships with you. The choices that you will make and the actions that you will take demonstrate that the chips will always be on the little pronoun, me.

Michelle Obama was and is victimized by racist name-calling and comments about her appearance. "They go low, we go high." In the name of femininity, woman to woman, not one white woman stood up for her although she is educated. What does it matter how she looks? White women have lost their jobs due to comments on public media disrespecting Michelle Obama because of her looks. Where is the sisterhood? Why do "we" always need to go high? A teacher was fired over racist Facebook comments about Michelle Obama calling her a gorilla multiple times. "She is the worst example of a First Lady ever!" (Why?) Oh sorry, I meant gorilla not First Lady!" This poor gorilla, how is she going to function in the real world by not having her luxurious vacations paid for any more? She needs to focus on getting a total make over especially the hair (Why?) instead of planning vacations!" Sounds to me like jealousy and resentment because she is a paraprofessional compared to a Harvard-trained attorney who was the First Lady.

A white female mayor was forced to resign after a racist Facebook post about Michelle Obama. Beverly Whaling apologized for the posting which she says was not intended to be racist. Following Donald Trump's election, Whaling posted: "It will be refreshing to have a classy, beautiful, dignified First Lady in the White House. I'm tired of seeing an Ape in heels." Apparently, Ms. Whaling does not understand the definition of classy: of high class, rank or grade; stylish; admirably smart. (Dictionary.com) Mrs. Obama is a Harvard Law School graduate. She graduated magna cum laude from Princeton with a Bachelor of Arts degree majoring in Sociology and African American studies. Among her many accomplishments in corporate America, Michelle was Associate Dean of Student Services at the University of Chicago. There is no hint of scandal in her background. We've read no reports of any white women criticizing and protesting Melania Trump's qualifications for First Lady.

Michelle Obama spoke at the 30th Anniversary of the Women's Foundation of Colorado. A recent interview with Clover Hope published on Jezebel.com, Michelle Obama talks about the racism she faced as First Lady. When asked about becoming the first black First Lady, Obama spoke about the racism she experienced, "alluding to being compared to an ape, among other things. 'The shards that cut me the deepest were the ones that were intended to cut.' Knowing that after 8 years of working really hard for this country, there are still people who won't see me for what I am because of my skin color." She doesn't pretend the attacks did not hurt her. She and her husband made the decision, "they go low, we go high." What a sacrifice.

Tamron Hall is labelled "difficult" because she chose to leave a daytime news show rather than be overlooked by executives who favored the white Megyn Kelly. Tamron has been called cutthroat. She well may be, but Megyn Kelly is not labelled as such. Is Tamron's display of displeasure by choosing to leave a lucrative position cutthroat or healthy self-respect? To hire Megyn Kelly without a plan for her then cancel a popular African American co-host is an insult. Any time an African American woman in corporate America dares display any dissatisfaction, she is labelled difficult.

Mary, who was recently transferred to West Computing, an area new to her, was looking for a rest room. Mary saw a group of white women standing in a group, "Can you direct me to the bathroom?" Mary asked the white women. The white women responded with giggles. How would "they" know where "her" bathroom was? The nearest bathroom was unmarked indicating that any white woman could use it. Restrooms for colored use were marked as such. The proximity to professional equality was the humiliating factor. We don't want you and we are not the reason that you are having problems. Mary Jackson is a woman who went on to become a mathematician and engineer. Yet she suffered this indignity.

Mom was a straight A student in high school. The

problem with Mom as she perceived it, she was a dark-skinned female who did not graduate high school. She always felt self-conscious until convinced to get her GED which she easily earned in the early 1980's. Reading various obituaries of women of that era, many teachers and nurses worked in their respective professions without formal education. Mom and other African American women were relegated to cleaning white women's homes while the white women enjoyed professional status. Intelligence was not the issue. Was the issue racial? Until African American women and white American women can call all things by their proper names race will remain an issue.

We are considered angry black women if we dare express any concern about any issue; however, a popular television show featuring an angry white woman, is a billionaire who is far angrier than we are. She portrays a rude, insolent, obnoxious and condescending woman but is paid billions of dollars for displaying the angry personae. African American women are expected to wear a smile at all times or else be viewed as something wrong. Something is wrong with us; not with them. Why? Are white women afraid we know and understand their real feelings toward us?

We have received no monetary inheritance from the bonds of slavery that has influenced our lives all the way to the present day. We do not feel included in your celebrations that do not reflect our heritage. We are not angry women, we are women who hurt, women who have been traumatized, women who have been devalued, and women who have been socially degraded and women who need to be validated. We don't want to concentrate on our likenesses when our differences are ignored. Our legacy is who we are: descendants of former slaves. Spend some time listening to what we have to say, not telling us what to say. Recognize our attributes and stop pretending they don't exist. We know that look you are mouthing the B word. We know that look, shocked that we have traveled abroad. We know that look, surprised she is that intelligent. It is the same look that said we were going to be sold down the river in slavery?

Look for things that we have in common instead of differences which usually means forget about our traditions and accept yours as the norm. We see the fear on your face when a racial issue comes up in conversation. We see padded conversations with interracial marriages; don't say anything because it may offend the white sister in-law, girl friend or daughter in-law.

A tenth-grade African American teen sitting in home economics, overheard a conversation about what day it was, St. Patrick's Day, a feast day celebrating both cultural and religious tradition, the patron saint of Ireland. Everyone had on green. The African American girl said she heard the PA announcement asking everyone to wear green apparel, but she forgot. The white (Irish) girl asked the African American girl why she would wear green; "you're not Irish." That is the point exactly. White folks do not wear dashikis in black history month.

African American women are their own unique beings. Our self-identity is treated like a strange phenomenon. We are different from island women, we are different from African women, we are different from Asian women, we are different from Latino women, we are different from brown women, we are different from Native American women, but we are different from white American women because we were not exempt from the horrors of your slavery. Psalm 133:1 says, "Behold, how good and how pleasant it is for brethren to dwell together in unity! Is it us or is it you?

Two middle-aged African American women were walking through an upscale mall, one with her expensive authentic Louis Vuitton bag on her shoulder and the other with an affordable luxury bag, Coach, on her shoulder. These women garnered outright looks of hatred and disdain from the faces of white women. Why do African American women attract so much attention? Is it their "good looks", the natural hair styles; the neat appearance-appropriate amount of make-up, modest hair styles or colors, no body piercings, no tattoos? Or is it that familiar look of "what are you doing here? Where did you get that handbag? How can you afford that handbag? You don't belong here."

It is interesting because as two middle-aged African American women, why do these women warrant your attention? Why can't they go unnoticed just as many other shoppers pass by? These white women are the same women who become our co-workers, managers, and hiring managers. Does this attitude present a bias?

From Bitter Root to Flower of Forgiveness: "I didn't mean to grow up bitter, but some people treated me without love because of my skin color. Calling me names, making fun of me. Turning me away. Closing their doors. In school, one teacher refused to call on me in class for an entire year. She called me "nobody" making it clear how little she thought of me. Laws in my country stopped me from using certain water fountains, restrooms, restaurants, or living in certain neighborhoods. In no time at all, I grew bitter. -----------Everyone around me hated people, I learned hate from them. I taught hate to others. What a tragic outcome that bitterness multiplies like a bad seed sprouting yet more ugly wrong."

CHAPTER 4

WHITE AMERICAN WOMEN PRIVILEGE, BLACK AMERICA WOMEN BURDEN

What is cunning in the kitten may be cruel in the cat. -R.U. Johnson, Daphne

White American Women Privilege,
Black America Women Burden

White women privilege is the acceptance of the idea that white women are rewarded with a vast array of benefits and advantages not privy to African American Women. This privilege is awarded because of their "whiteness" alone and not on any talent or ability of those thus privileged.

We have read about the women's right to vote marches (suffrages) which did not include African American women. We remember the women's lib movement march with women taking off and burning their bras and now the 2017 women's march on Washington (The nasty women's march). Have these efforts really created a bond between African American women and white American women? Some women will say there is no conflict, we are all women if we just concentrate on how we are alike versus our differences. When we all strip down we have the same body parts. Is that enough? Marching for equal pay for women does not necessarily apply to African American women because we get lower pay than white men and women because of the color of our skin, not because we are women. We don't have a period in history that we have not worked. We worked as slaves, we worked as share croppers, we worked as maids, we worked as domestics, we worked as nannies, we worked in factories, and we worked in textile mills. We worked as cooks before chefs and cooking shows became popular. Betty Friedan's take on the modern feminist movement was not meant for working class women or women of color who already worked outside the home. Ms. Friedan's focus was white, middle-class women who aspired to the workplace.

Black American women have been absorbed into everyone's movements. The civil rights movement has become the equal rights for everyone movement.

We need to question our assumptions about marching in protest for rights and involving ourselves in movements. We as black women assume women's rights include us. While we are included in the broadest sense; i.e., any legislation enacted, by and large all women are included. This is a residual benefit that has nothing specifically to do with black women.

We are a polarized society. Some women marched for equal pay, some march for LGTB rights, some marched for the right to have an abortion but no one marched to have bonding and open dialogue for African American women and white women. It is not politically correct to distinguish ourselves as African American women, but to be included and lost into women of color. Is it because it doesn't include the brown women, the Latino women, the Native American women or is because it is not politically correct or is it to exclude the black women?

The nasty women's march was organized by and for white women but committed to the inclusion of all women. The event founder, Bob Bland, a white woman, recognized that women of color (African American women) needed to be part of the planning to gain the support of other nonwhite women. Including African American women and other women of color is self-serving. Adding women of color to organizers helped give the march credibility along with its policy platform. Black women are striving to ensure they are not used as tokens but are involved in policy making front and center.

Interestingly, after women of color were brought on board in leadership positions for the nasty women's march, some white women backed out of the march. A white woman said she felt "unwelcome" when confronted with black and brown women who expected white women to accept their own role in the oppression of non-white women. Again, anytime a black woman dares to speak about how we feel, white women do not like our tone, or they become fearful.

At the beginning of the suffrage movement, black women were forced to march separately in the suffrage parade. The book, "The History of Women's Suffrage" by Elizabeth Cady Stanton and Susan B. Anthony in the 1880's, overlooked contributions of black suffragists. Anthony is quoted as stating, "I will cut off this right arm of mine before I will ever work or demand the ballot for the Negro and not the women." While claiming to fight for voting rights, Anthony did not want black men to get the vote before white women. Nowhere is the black woman even mentioned. Black reformers organized their own groups. Black women founded The National Association of Colored Women in 1896. The black suffragists focused not only on voting rights, but other issues affecting the black community.

While doing college tours with my grandson, I was amazed that one biology department at a state university speaker said that their faculty was very diverse. When pictures were put up on the screen there was not one African American. There were white females, one brown person, white males and the speaker was of Asian descent. My first thought was they have excluded us from diversity and white women were included because they were under represented in the work force. However, there is a great disparity in the health, wealth, and education of African Americans and this continues to expand. Being an African American female can be a life sentence of exclusion, not a diverse inclusion.

At the women's march on Washington not a single protestor was arrested. That is great news. Is this incontrovertible proof that when women lead, peace follows? Hardly. Instead of simply priding ourselves, ladies, let's own what really happened: no one saw our majority-white-female bodily presence as a threat requiring containment. Another photo circulated of three white women in pink hats smiling into their own phones near a black woman holding a sign reminding us that many white women voted for Trump. The image has been divisive. That sign does not state an alternative fact — nor should we ignore that 94% of black women voted against Trump. These things are simply true. Just as our march was given the benefit of the doubt by law enforcement. "Surely no one in public relations would be a fan of the optics of men in uniform roughing up a mass of white ladies." Sometimes. It's case-dependent, and often requires one to notice it in a certain context. It's hard to tell that a paint swatch is eggshell until a white swatch is held up against it. To realize where you stand in the ladder of privilege, you need to see the other rungs. I also realize that there are many privileges; deep, societal ones, that I may never come to notice.

White women played a significant role in electing a racist, misogynist to the presidency. "Mainstream feminism has focused for decades, on making women more politically and individually powerful, and almost no energy in thinking about how to cut through white women's allegiance to the racist, patriarchal systems that value them." But why would they since a high value is placed on white womanhood. Loyalty to the status quo exists. The white woman's power lies in maintaining the status quo. Their power depends upon the exclusion of people of color. There is a "dichotomy throughout history between patriarchy and sisterhood – They chose patriarchy."

According to CNN, 53% of white females voted for Donald Trump. White women voted on the side of white men. They decided defending their position of power as white people was more important than the rest of the world of whom Trump maligned. White women identify more with white men than with women of color; black or any other ethnicity. White women sold out fellow women and themselves. White women sold out the sisterhood by Voting for Trump.

White women chose the protection of their whiteness over the solidarity of womanhood. They identified more with white men than with all other groups of women. Black women fought for a candidate (Clinton) who they were not sure would fight for them, where white women voted for a candidate that made it clear he would not fight for women and that did not matter to our fellow womanhood. Our issues are ignored or sidelined. White women do not possess a sense of justice.

The original nasty women's march of 2017 for the most part represented women's dissatisfaction with the Trump administration and women's rights. The 2018 march focus shifted to immigration rights and Deferred Action for Childhood Arrivals (DACA). While women's rights are a concern to and for all women, immigration targets specific groups; benefits to some groups (illegal) and exclusion to other groups; specifically, illegals versus those from African related countries and ethnicities.

With all the focus on DACA related issues, where is the outcry for black Americans whose ancestors were brought here against their will and generations later are black American legal citizen? How can illegal immigrants demand rights in a country where they are not citizens? How do illegal immigrants manage more rights than legal citizens, specifically black Americans? The black agenda is once again eclipsed. Do human rights extend to African Americans?

White feminist's early failures to embrace black women in the Suffrage Movement set the stage for future decades of exclusion that still make it difficult to join them in solidarity. From slavery to suffrage to the 21st century, there exists a chasm. There is no unity or solidarity between African American women and white American women.

White American Women's Privilege

1. I have had the privilege of being respected by the police.
2. I have had the privilege of attending the best schools.
3. I have had the privilege of seeing my race dominate television viewing.
4. I have had the privilege of not having negative stereotypes associated with my race.
5. I have had the privilege of not accepting any ownership of centuries of racial history.
6. I have had the privilege of not being stopped by a policeman for driving a luxury car.
7. I have had the privilege of being treated leniently by the courts.
8. I have had the privilege of not being burdened with the daily harshness of racism.
9. I have the privilege of shopping freely and not being followed in stores.
10. I have had the privilege of expecting favoritism as my birth right.
11. **Above all, I have the privilege of my whiteness.**

Black America Women's Burden

1. I have had the burden of having my sons and husbands killed by your sons and husbands.
2. I have had the burden of attending the worse schools.
3. I have had the burden of not seeing my race dominate television viewing.
4. I have had the burden of having negative stereotypes associated with my race.
5. I have had the burden of accepting any ownership of centuries of racial history.
6. I have had the burden of being stopped by a policeman for driving a luxury car.
7. I have had the burden of not being treated leniently by the courts.
8. I have had the burden of being burdened with the daily harshness of racism.
9. I have the burden of not shopping freely and being followed in stores.
10. I have had the burden of not expecting favoritism as my birth right.
11. **Above all, I have the burden of my black skin.**

Existing as a black woman in America can be a daunting and often fatal experience. Black women and girls make up 13 percent of the U.S. population yet account for 33 percent of all women killed by police, according to the African American Policy Forum. At least two of the five black women killed in 2017 were pregnant, according to a tracker of police shootings from The Washington Post. Charleena Lyles, 30, was shot and killed by two Seattle police officers on June 18. Alteria Woods, 21, was shot and killed on March 19 during a SWAT team raid at her boyfriend's apartment in Gifford, Florida. Authorities claimed Woods' boyfriend used her as a human shield during the shootout. Seattle police says Lyles was killed after she lunged at officers with a knife.

Police also have a history of roughing up pregnant black women. In 1992, Delois Young, at the time eight months pregnant, was shot by a California sheriff's deputy during an illegal raid on her home. She survived; the fetus was killed. Starr Brown, a pregnant woman from East Baltimore, was choked and slammed face down on the sidewalk by an officer in 2009. Charlena Michelle Cooks was eight months pregnant when two officers pinned her stomach-first against a chain-link fence in Barstow, California, in 2015.

"Maternal mortality for black women is an epidemic level," said Marcela Howell, the founder and executive director of In Our Own Voice and Huffington Post contributor. "It cuts across all economic levels and all educational levels. We are not just talking about poor black women. Black women should not be afraid. . .if they call the police for help," she said.

What about the corporate white woman? What about her? She's all smiles, friendly, full of compliments. But. . .we all know not to trust that smile. Let her know **ANYTHING** at all about you and off she goes telling everyone. Whispering. Off to the boss reporting, especially if what she's reporting will benefit her and make you look bad.

Subterfuge. A white woman will undermine you, all with a smile on her face. After undermining you, even taking your job or becoming your boss, she will cheerfully give you directions. **AND** if you dare to speak up, complain or look unhappy, "what's wrong," "is something bothering you?" Next thing you know you are in HR or worse yet fired, for insubordination. That is when the triumphant gloat appears. Too late for you, you black woman.

Sitting at my desk, a white female executive came by to speak with the executive I supported. We made small talk, and suddenly she confided in me about a very personal matter. I was taken aback because, although we made friendly conversation, she knew nothing about me other than I was well thought of by my manager and other managers on the floor. I pondered why she would confide in me, someone she barely knew. I am known for my ability to maintain a confidence and then it occurred to me it was a TRAP!! She confided in me to find out if I could maintain juicy gossip. Of course, her confidence was not broken, but this incident demonstrates the deceptive, racist views held by some white women, with a smile no less. Subterfuge. Black women are held in contempt.

In the corporate world, I was well thought of by management; able to maintain confidentiality, attentive to detail, trustworthy. I hear complimentary remarks again and again. The feeling was mutual on a professional level. The executives were very kind, understanding and fair. Generous with praise, performance appraisals and bonuses, in addition to bringing in various gifts, I felt appreciated. I was even invited to their homes as well as luncheons on various occasions.

In the corporate world, I honed the inter-personal skills of attention to detail, trustworthiness, dependability and the ability to maintain confidentiality. My performance reviews were always excellent. I worked hard to elevate these skills in addition to any technical skills by taking advantage of corporate training and additional formal education. Yet with this reputation I was never been offered opportunities for advancement.

This calls to question, why? Is it the fundamental issue that I am a black woman? I notice white women are offered opportunities or even have positions created for them. Research shows that we tend to "like" (favor) those that look like us. Some would argue that it is unconscious bias. I wonder if I was just the "good little house nigger" in my effort to do a good job, stay out of office politics and display loyalty.

At one interview, the interviewer and I jelled instantly. Instant rapport. During the interview, I was "given" the position. I was told I would present well. What does present well mean? After seeing the other employees in similar positions, I realized we all looked alike; the colored ones, that is. We all had medium/long hair, medium brown complexion; enough color to say, "Look, we are not prejudiced. Just look around." Not dark enough to offend their white sensibilities. One white woman told me she liked me because I wasn't dark like some of them. Some of who? My ancestors, my sisters, my friends?

Performance reviews were excellent. Individual effort in education and self-improvement did not result in advancement. I was repeatedly overlooked. Could it be, as a friend said, "you weren't deemed worthy of it (promotion/advancement)." Apparently, my friend was correct. I was not deemed worthy of advancement. I have observed this situation with other African American women. Although continual effort at self-improvement and adding value is made, African American women are routinely overlooked for advancement.

Though black women co-habit the "big house," in many cases, the white woman is still valued more than the black woman (African American, colored woman) of equal or greater qualifications.

CHAPTER 5

DIVERSITY

Sometimes, I feel discriminated against, but it does not make me angry. It merely astonishes me. How can any deny themselves the pleasure of my company? It's beyond me. -Zora Neale Hurston

Merriam Webster Dictionary defines diversity as the condition of having or being composed of differing elements: variety; especially the inclusion of different types of people (as people of different races or cultures) in a group or organization programs intended to promote **diversity** in schools. The state or fact of being **diverse**; difference; unlikeness: ... the inclusion of individuals representing more than one national origin, color, religion, socioeconomic stratum, sexual orientation. Diversity means understanding that individuals are unique and recognizing our individual differences. Differences can be racial, ethnicity, gender, sexual orientation, socio-economic status, age, physical abilities, religious beliefs, political beliefs, or other ideologies and characteristics.

Organizations are recognized for diversity. Since the definition of diversity is so broad, let's look at a corporation at the executive level. One or two black males, one or two black women, a few white males, with the remainder and majority, white women. Is this true diversity or just another strategy to keep the wealth in the white household? The broadness surrounding the definition of diversity allows, once again, the black female to be edged out. Corporations will always have at least one black face to demonstrate their diversity; however, it is white women that make up the majority of the "diverse" corporate environment.

White women hold approximately 40% of the middle management positions; black women 5%; black men 4%. "Privilege is not something white women take; therefore, have no option to not take. It is something bestowed upon them by society." These white women possess "unearned power conferred systematically."

The ability to change diversity is mind boggling. Child care had always been black women's territory to look after white children because of low pay. However, when Head Start and day care came onboard in the sixties, black women quickly became unable to care for children. Child care workers had to become fully qualified degreed teachers. New curriculum and early childhood development programs were established. Suddenly white women don't trust black women to take care of their children. If we were so incompetent, why were we taking care of your children in the first place?

Some black women have always been fat and wore large sized clothes. An epiphany, white women are fat too; however, society characterizes them as curvy necessitating plus size clothes. Black women's issues with weight have historically been due, in part, to the lack of availability of healthy foods. Slave owners often gave slaves scraps for food; the fatty pieces and skin. Sometimes the food was spoiled. To make food palatable, excess salt and/or sugar and fat were added to enhance flavor.

The Smithsonian magazine, in an article entitled, "The Genetics of Taste" cites genetic memory as a factor in black women's food preferences which directly impacts not only weight and body size but health. We are exposed to taste in the womb and through breast milk. If the mother's diet is nutritionally poor, that will affect not only the physical health but the food choices of a person.

Modern black Americans often live in areas defined as food deserts. Fresh produce and lean cuts of meat are unavailable in neighborhoods. If one has no transportation, the choices are limited to what is available; packaged, processed foods high in sodium, fat, sugar and artificial flavorings and colorings. All these ingredients are known to have a detrimental impact on health and on the waist line.

Keep in mind, however, that many of the conditions that result in obesity in black women, have a direct correlation to racism in America. From slavery to the current education and employment process, all impact obesity and overall health. Yet white America turns around and uses the results of their racist tactics against black America as though it is the black's fault instead of a result of their racist policies. White America creates the issue then uses the issue that was created against black America (women).

In 1984, Jessie Jackson gave a speech before the Democratic National Convention. "We must all come together. . .When one of us rises, we all rise" (referring to Native Americans, Hispanic Americans, African Americans, women, children, former workers, LGBT populations). In theory, this statement is true; however, when one class oppresses another for their own economic advantage, we all cannot and do not rise. As I was listening to this speech, while it sounded good, I realized that once all these groups became involved in the civil rights movement, African American's rights would once again be relegated to a position of lesser importance. That is what has happened.

Coretta Scott King wrote a letter warning of the threat liberal immigration laws pose to black workers. Written in 1991 to Republican Senator Orrin Hatch, King argued for enforcement of immigration laws. The concern was that Hatch's proposal to remove sanctions on employers who hired illegals would cause another problem; discrimination against minority American (black) workers in favor of cheaper illegal immigrant workers. Her prediction became reality for a period when black service industry employees were displaced for cheap illegal immigrant labor. Again, black American's agenda set aside.

CHAPTER 6

BONDING AND RELATIONSHIPS

Not what we give, but what we share, for
the gift without the giver is bare.
-J.R. Lowell, Vision of Sir Launfal, II

Bonding and relationships **are** simple concepts, or are they? Bonding is defined as an idea, interest, experience or feeling that is shared between people or groups, a uniting, binding, bridge, connection, interrelationship, relationship, linked with synonyms like adherence and guarantee. Relationship can be even easier to understand. It is definable as the way in which two or more concepts, objects or people are connected. Relationship has synonyms such as connection, relations, association, link, correlation, alliance, and bond and inter connection. Think about what areas fit the African American and white American women's relationship.

One of the earliest Christian poems in English literature is "The Dream of the Rood." In this old English poem, the rood refers to the Cross on which Christ was crucified. When the tree learns that it is to be used to kill the son of God he rejects the idea of being used in that way, but Christ enlists the help of the tree to provide for all who believe. Our trees don't talk for we do not really know each other. Where is our turning point? When you look at our children in the strollers do you see little baby maids, little baby janitors, little baby fast food workers, little baby criminals, little baby drug addicts or do you see as we see little baby doctors, little baby attorneys, little baby scientist, little baby NASA computer engineers? A question was asked by a white American woman. How did the black African American women who worked at NASA get so smart? Oh my! They were born that way. Surprise, surprise! We are braver than you believe we are. We are stronger than we seem. We are tougher than you thought we were and surprisingly we are also smarter than you thought we were. Most of us have an image of ourselves that we want others to have of us.

None of us want our image to be created by someone else. We desire and deserve to be accurately portrayed. How does a white American female know how to portray a black African American woman? What portrait are white women painting?

CHAPTER 7

HARMONY AND DYSFUNCTION

Hating people is like burning down your
own house to get rid of a rat.
-Harry Emerson Fosdick, The Wages of Hate

Harmony usually refers to the following well known list: agreement, accord, peace, peacefulness, amity, amicability, friendship, fellowship, cooperation, understanding, consensus, unity, sympathy, rapport and like-minded. However, harmony develops when we tend to each other's personal needs with no strings attached and we remember to recognize each other as allies not enemies. For the most part, African American women and white American women do not have a harmonious relationship because the above elements are not in existence. Often, we don't agree, we are not amicable, there is no peacefulness, there are no friendships, we don't cooperate, we don't understand each other, we have no consensus. Unity doesn't exist, sympathy is null and void. There is no rapport and most of all we are not like minded.

The Daughters of the American Revolution (DAR) is a lineage-based membership service organization for women who are directly descended from a person involved in the United States struggle for independence. For years racism and the control of history have kept African American women out of the Daughters of the American Revolution. It is a low estimate that only about 5,000 of the nearly 40,000 American soldiers in the Revolution war were black. Eric Grundset, director of the organization's library, states that some were free slaves, who joined voluntarily, other were slaves who bartered their services against promises of earning their freedom (which was often reneged on), and others were sent to fight in place of the men who owned them.

The word **dysfunctional** is often used to describe, relationships. Functional usually refers to properly working order; dysfunctional is the opposite. Something is broken, out of order, not working properly and unable to do what it was designed to do. A functional relationship is the key to understanding one another. We are normally not functional because there is a sense of mistrust.

March 19, 1935 in New York a black youth suspected of shopping lifting had been struck by a white policeman on 125th street and a riot started. Blacks went into the streets dramatizing the event of a brutal murder. Looters roamed the streets breaking store windows, attacking buses and shouting at police. Seventy-nine years later we see these types of incidents replay themselves.

The shooting of Michael Brown occurred on August 9, 2014, in Ferguson, Missouri, a northern suburb of St. Louis. Brown, an 18-year-old black man, was fatally shot by Darren Wilson, 28, a white Ferguson police officer, after reportedly robbing a convenience store. The circumstances of the shooting, which were initially disputed, sparked existing tensions in the predominantly black city, where protests and civil unrest erupted. The events received considerable attention in the U.S. and elsewhere, attracting protesters from outside the region. They generated a vigorous national debate about the relationship between law enforcement and African Americans, and about police use-of-force doctrine in Missouri and nationwide. A St. Louis County grand jury decided not to indict Wilson, and he was exonerated of criminal wrongdoing by the United States Department of Justice. Why would Africans American women not be concerned in 2017 about what happened before most of them were born? We have our own life's experiences. They are as real to us today as they were yesterday. To ask us to forget is an excuse for taking no action in 1935.

In 1705 The Virginia Code of law removed criminal consequences for killing a slave in the act of correcting him_____ and if any slave resist (sic) his master, owner or other person by his or her order, correcting such slave, and shall happen to be killed in such correction, it shall not be accounted a felony but the master, owner and every other person so giving correction, shall be free and acquit (sic) of all punishment and accusation for the same, as such accident had never happened. Malice could not be presumed. This code was also referred to as "The Casual Killing Act." Babies born to slave rape victims were beheaded by the slave master's wife. Slave babies were used as alligator bait. "Casual Killing Law" forgave white women for beating our babies to death over minor infractions like spilling a drink. The Casual Killing Law remained on law books in some states until 1985.

Though the law may no longer be on the books, the spirit of the law lives on in white America. White police officers are repeatedly not charged or acquitted of killing "unarmed blacks." This is an endorsement to kill blacks with no consequences, "no malice presumed" in 2017.

Is the justifiable homicide of today the modern-day casual killing of slaves? Defining African American enslaved people as "slaves" dehumanizes the enslaved. "Slaves" in America are human beings who were enslaved based on skin color and ethnicity. The term slave suggests a sub-group less than human. This emboldens ones to treat African Americans as something less than human rather than an enslaved people.

Recently, an Atlanta, Georgia homeless woman was beaten mercilessly for non-compliance with a police officer. The woman was already on the floor, the officer's knee in her back, yet he continued to beat her about the head. The officer clearly weighed at least twice as much as the woman. The incident was captured on film. After investigating, internal affairs found that the beating was justifiable and according to training; however, the new white female chief of police feels that such beating is not justifiable. Perhaps, the chief's attitude will lead to positive change in how police officers handle citizens (black women included).

CHAPTER 8

EMPATHY

Dr. Mary McLeod Bethune believed that women were the major key to change. "We are indebted to women, first for life itself and then for making it worth having."

Empathy, defined as the capacity to understand or feel what another person is experiencing from within the other person's frame of reference and the capacity to place oneself in another's position. Empathy is part of your character. Character is who you are inside.

Rebecca Epstein, lead author and executive director for the center and Jamilia J. Blake, co-author and an associate professor at Texas A&M University, defined adultification as viewing African American girls as less innocent than white counterparts. One reason this might be occurring is because black girls are being held to the same stereotypes as of black women are held to. Blake said, "Black women have been historically and currently seen as being aggressive, loud, defiant and over sexualized. I believe, along with many other researchers, that the stereotypes of black women are being mapped on to black girls. With this mapping, little girls are being set up to be torn down by the same skewed and bigoted standards their mothers have been held to.

"A new report found that adults view young black girls as less innocent and more adult- like than white girls starting as young as 5 years old." Why should a little black girl age five be burdened with how she is viewed by adults? Although it is the mindset of the adult who has such views, it is how she will be viewed for the rest of her life. The Huffington Post reports entitled: Girlhood Interrupted: The Erasure of Black Girls' Childhood," shows that society's perception of black girls leads to their "adultification." It was reported that adults believed that black girls seemed older than white girls of the same age, and think that black girls need less nurturing, protection, support and comfort than white girls. It also found that people assumed black girls are more independent, know more about adult topics and know more about sex than young white girls.

The report which built on information from a 2014 study by Phillip Goff that found that black boys are more likely to be viewed as older and suspected of crimes starting at age 10- is the first of its kind to focus on girls. Researchers surveyed 325 adults from racial and ethnic backgrounds in a ratio that mirrors the country's population. Many of the adults surveyed had a high school diploma or higher. The greatest differences were found in ways adults view children in the age brackets 5-9 and 10-14. These differences continued to a lesser degree in the 15-19 age bracket.

As an African American woman, I love assisting children of all ethnicities with their studies. In addition, I try to inject social skills, manners and appropriateness when the occasion arises. One trend I notice among African American girls is inappropriate "twerking," hands in their underwear, etc. I most always inform them of the inappropriateness of their behavior. I speak to them if I can do so without embarrassing them or sometimes a simple head shake will do. On the occasions when I mention their behavior, the white women look surprised. I notice the white women do not correct this unbecoming behavior. White women give me a quizzical look. This an example for setting African American girls up for failure. Most often those displaying these behaviors are not performing well in their lessons. Their attention needs to be directed to appropriate behavior and lessons.

It has been stated, "You make a living by what you get but you make a life by what you give." Women have an awareness of our position in a relationship with other women. We know that a balance must always be maintained to keep a relationship alive and active. To have this balance there must be unity. To have unity, empathy is needed and a recognition of interdependence. When these things are not in place, the whole order is upset. The upset will not foster peace and harmony. A lack of empathy for black women reaches back as far as biblical times. "And Miriam and Aaron spoke against Moses because of the Ethiopian woman he had married, and the anger of the Lord was kindled against them." (Numbers 12:1-9) In America, a system for inequality was set for eternity way back in slavery and the lack of empathy has been fostered generation after generation. The name for it may have changed but it is still inequality and lack of empathy.

CHAPTER 9

BLACK MEN, WHITE WOMEN

They want everything but the burden. -Fannie Davis

Ain't I a Woman? (Sojourner Truth)

"Ain't I a Woman?" as recounted by Frances Gage, in 1863

Well, children, where there is so much racket there must be something out of kilter. I think that 'twixt the negroes of the South and the women at the North, all talking about rights, the white men will be in a fix pretty soon. But what's all this here talking about?

That man over there says that women need to be helped into carriages, and lifted over ditches, and to have the best place everywhere. Nobody ever helps me into carriages, or over mud-puddles, or gives me any best place! And isn't I a woman? Look at me! Look at my arm! I have ploughed and planted, and gathered into barns, and no man could head me! And isn't I a woman? I could work as much and eat as much as a man–when I could get it–and bear the lash as well! And isn't I a woman? I have borne thirteen children, and seen most all sold off to slavery, and when I cried out with my mother's grief, none but Jesus heard me! And ain't I a woman?

Then they talk about this thing in the head; what's this they call it? [Member of audience whispers, "Intellect"] That's it, honey. What's that got to do with women's rights or Negroes' rights? If my cup won't hold but a pint, and yours holds a quart, wouldn't you be mean not to let me have my little half measure full?

Then that little man in black there, he says women can't have as much rights as men, because Christ wasn't a woman! Where did your Christ come from? Where did your Christ come from? From God and a woman! Man had nothing to do with Him.

If the first woman God ever made was strong enough to turn the world upside down all alone, these women together ought to be able to turn it back and get it right side up again! And now they is (sic) asking to do it, the men better let them.

Obliged to you for hearing me, and now old Sojourner ain't got nothing more to say.

As reported in the *Anti-Slavery Bugle*, Salem, Ohio, June 21, 1851

Black men, White women

Clarence Thomas	$715,000 – $1.8 million
Louis Gates	$1 million
Michael Jordan	$1 billion
Frederick Douglas	N/A
Scotty Pippins	$45 million
Michael Strahan	$35 million
Bryant Gumbel	$18 million
Kanye West	$160 million
Romeo	$5 million
Tiger Woods	$740 million
Sidney Poitier	$65 million
Quincy Jones	$400 million
Lamar Odom	$56 million
James Earl Jones	$45 million
Evan Ross	$20 million
Charles Barkley	$40 million
Cuba Gooding, Jr.	$15 million
Alfonso Ribeiro	$7 million
Lester Holt	$12 million
Kobe Bryant	$350 million
Russell Simmons	$340 million
Reggie Bush	$14 million
Harry Belafonte	$28 million
Tiki Barber	$18 million
Robert Smith (billionaire equity funds)	$3.3 billion
Robert Griffin III	$10 million
Craig Melvin	$700,000
Taye Diggs	$16 million
Dr. Dre	$740 million

Ice T	$35 million
Tim Duncan	$130 million
John Legend	$40 million
Dwayne "The Rock" Johnson	$256 million
Hank Baskett	$6.5 million
Charlie Wilson	$15 million
Jamie Foxx	$85 million

At the end, what do they all have in common, white wives. In terms of generational wealth, this represents a $8,032,000,000 (8 billion 32 million plus) loss to the black community.

According to the Daily Mail.com, Nicki Minaj took issue with Kanye West for the lyrics in his tune, "Gold Digger". The lyrics say, in part, "When he get on, (meaning when he becomes successful) he will leave your ass for a white girl. . ." Kanye's lyrical line states what is generally accepted as fact.

Minaj is also said to be incensed about Kanye's white wife, Kim Kardashian's nude selfies. The public praised Kardashian while Minaj was ridiculed and insulted for doing the same thing. Kardashian was not labelled as trashy and raunchy as was Minaj. The double standard applies; anything a white woman does is acceptable, but a black woman can do the exact same thing and must endure ridicule and shaming.

An anonymous writer posing as an athlete said black athletes with money do not marry black women because black women are argumentative and stubborn. A personal acquaintance relating a couple's break up to me said, ". . .he left her (his black wife) for a white woman." I understood that was supposed to be the ultimate insult suggesting that the white woman was of more value than the black woman and that he had finally attained the prize.

Why do black men perceive white women as more beautiful, sensuous, and submissive than black women? Apparently, black and mulatto men marry white women to improve their social status. To these men, it is necessary to have a fancy car, fancy lifestyle and a white woman. Some say black men are tired of "black women drama." Is this due to media portrayal of white women as ever beautiful versus the angry black women? The standard set for beauty has been based on the European standard of blonde haired and blue eyed. European beauty is the epitome of what is good and right. The media has done a good job of selling the white woman and a poor job selling the black woman. Black men's self-esteem is heightened by having a white woman; disregarding who birthed him or what the white woman looks like. The black woman has been portrayed negatively in the media. Black women receive awards for portraying victims of rape, abuse, prostitution and drug abuse. The language is cleaned up for white women. It is now human trafficking. The black woman has been given such titles as angry, gold digger, male basher, sapphire, and bitch, and known to be hard to get along with.

The media always describes white women as beautiful no matter how they look. Really? All of them? Beautiful black women are not described as beautiful. They are described as sexy or exotic, never beautiful. This portrayal reinforces the Jezebel, sex crazed black woman image.

The reality shows have set black women back a hundred years. The women who participate are missing an important fact; money does not equate to class. If you are a queen no one need ask if you are a queen. Queens are defined by their actions. You are validating the media portrayal of being trashy. A black man with class would not take you home to meet his mother nor would he take a trashy white woman. He knows the difference. Then why do the number of black men that are married to white women far outnumber all other cross-cultural marriages. Subconsciously, black men believe they are getting what society considers the best. Beauty is not a consideration as some highly educated African American men have unattractive white wives. Black women see it as a slap in the face and a monetary rape of the black community. It takes away generational wealth from the black community. It raids the opportunity for black families to advance in society. Gone are the days where black men were taught that they not only represent their family but they also represent their race. A racial divide has been drawn. Black women are commanding respect and support from our men.

The media has a direct impact on how black women are perceived. On a trip to London, a black sales clerk asked where I was from and I replied Atlanta. The clerk asked if all the women in Atlanta act like the women portrayed on television and in the media. My response was that clearly some women do act like that and some do not. However, this is the image of black women projected around the world; money grabbing, cat fighting, deceitful, promiscuous behavior. Television shows that do not support this image of black women and the black family such as blackish are not as widely viewed or successful. Blackish portrays a professional black woman as an anesthesiologist, married to an executive black man who faces challenges of life just as any other family of any ethnicity would.

Where are white women degraded for displaying their bare breasts or bottoms? Black women are often portrayed with breasts bared and labelled as savages. White women voluntarily display their bodies for the world to see and are rewarded and applauded for that behavior in the media; Kim Kardashian for one.

CHAPTER 10

NEW TRENDS

**If you want people to believe you, appeal
to their heart not their brains.**
-Bangambik Habyarimana

Is it me, Is it my hair, Is it my skin color, is it my eyes, or is it you?

The new trend, because you have a black husband, you want to be in our organizations. Not only do you want to be in our organizations, you want to join and then take control of the organization. You don't have a clue who we are and what we do. You have not educated yourself about the organization's mission, goal and purpose. You just waltz in attempting to set the agenda. You demand concessions be made to accommodate your beliefs and traditions. You forget that it is our organization you joined.

Folks usually join organizations because of a common goal, a common background or a common purpose. Based on this commonality, the organization proceeds to set an agenda and traditions for the organization. So then, this begs the question, why have you, white woman, tried to commandeer our organizations? Is it because your white race has rejected you based on your black marriage partner? Or is this just another attempt to usurp any control black women may have?

Is it me, is it my hair, is it my skin
color, is it my eyes, or is it you?
We must all hang together or else
we shall all hang separately.
-Benjamin Franklin

CHAPTER 11

IS IT ME, IS IT MY HAIR, IS IT MY SKIN COLOR, IS IT MY EYES, OR IS IT YOU?

Having breast cancer is fearful and devastating to any female. You have a short time to process what is going on, because the sooner the disease is diagnosed, and surgery is done, the better your chances are for survival. I was one of the fortunate as well as the unfortunate. I had to have a mastectomy to be cancer free. A GYN told me years ago that when a body part is taken there is a mourning and healing period that may last a year or more. Your body must get used to not having the part that it was meant to have. You may have aches and pains or sensations in that area for years.

You learn to look appreciatively at little things like getting your first prosthesis, all pepped up and ready to get back in a bra. The nice white lady was to get me fitted for a prosthesis and choose some bras. Not knowing what to expect, I was excited to see what it looked like since I had never seen one. She opened the box and took out a very dark colored prosthesis that looked nothing like the color of my skin. I said do you have something that matches my skin tone? She said this is what the black women usually get. I said I would like for you to get one that matches my skin color which is closer to your color. After a huff she went and came back with one very close to my skin complexion. Out of the window went my little bit of joy. She saw me as her vision of an African American woman, not who I am. She saw me as being dark or she didn't care about my feelings; she only cared about her job. Was it an unfortunate incident? Maybe I thought, but every two years you can get a new prosthesis. I was at a different location to get a new prosthesis. Even though I had on a prosthesis that was my skin color, out of the box was a dark one again. No, I want my skin color; no exceptions.

I can't recall the multiple times I have been offered very dark makeup in department stores, even makeup designed for African American women. There is no consideration for variations of skin colors. I usually ask the makeup artist to rub it on her hand to see what she thinks. Is it my skin color or is it yours? Then there is the hair thing. So, many times I have lost count, I have been approached by white American women about my hair. Yes, this is my natural hair that curls into little ringlets when shampooed. I have been outright told by white women, no it's not your natural hair to the point they are arguing with me. How do you get your hair to look so pretty? Why do you want to know? We don't ask you in public, in stores or in the post office how you get your hair to look a certain way. We also don't argue with you about your answers. Why do you care? We resent you asking us about our hair and not accepting our answers. What is it with the hair thing? If you aren't asking us about our hair you are following us around in the store to make sure we aren't stealing hair products.

A California woman shopping at Walmart said she was shocked to find beauty products used by African-Americans shelved behind locked glass. Essie Grundy, 43, said it is the first time she's directly experienced racism, and she decided to file a racial discrimination lawsuit against Walmart. The product in question was a 49-cent comb she originally purchased with no problem at the Riverside Walmart, according to the lawsuit. Grundy said that when she went to her local Walmart in Perris, California she found the comb and other products used by African-Americans behind glass. "It was such a good product, I wanted to introduce it to my older children," Grundy said, according to KCBS. "They didn't have any more at the original Walmart that I got it from, so I went to my neighborhood Walmart, and that's when I noticed all of the African-American products were locked up under lock and key." She said she was shocked that the products would be locked away, and she asked a store manager to change the policy. The manager refused. Similar complaints have been made by groups such as Making Change at Walmart, which has described the lock-and-key policy as a "discriminatory practice." Grundy is being represented by women's rights attorney Gloria Allred, who said they're seeking a court injunction to halt Walmart's practice of locking up these products. Walmart spokesman, Charles Crowson, said in a statement that the company does not discriminate, but that it will review Grundy's complaint. He said some products, such as baby formula and razors, are more frequently targeted by shoplifters, and that certain products are kept locked because of a greater risk of theft. Walmart said in a statement to Business Insider that it does "not tolerate discrimination of any kind." "We're sensitive to this situation and understand like other retailers, that some products such as electronics, automotive, cosmetics and other personal care products are subject to additional security. Those determinations are made on a store-by-store basis using data supporting the need for the heightened measures," a Walmart spokesperson said. In the English language that means that there is a belief that black women steal more beauty products than white women. I wonder if they steal the dark colors.

If African American women recorded all their unpleasant incidents, we could not complete the task in a lifetime. Relationships between African American women and white

American women are like a huge family dinner. You spend hours in the kitchen preparing an elaborate meal and then you place it on the dining room table. However, you must understand the struggle that went into the preparation, you must sit, eat and share in order to build an understandable relationship. "We shouldn't bash or shame women of color for talking about their struggles, because that's being real, that's being human."

When a person happens to see themselves reflected in another person, the view of themselves becomes highly distorted because the image is not much different than their image. This recognition then becomes surreal and unacceptable. The recognition that the person is a lot like them becomes a reason to dislike that person because surely white American women are not like African American women. A whole culture then is based on fear of being like or unlike the other person. One can believe that their culture is superior by simply justifying a wrong opinion and declaring that it is correct. Straight hair is pretty and kinky hair is not. Therefore, your kinky hair can't be pretty. Then comes the question, how did you make it pretty?

I had always assumed that my eyes were brown. All medical records and other records said brown eyes; however, my eyes looked blue. I remember one doctor saying you have blue eyes. That is an indication that your cholesterol is elevated. Being that I wore glasses, designer glasses were more of an issue than the color of my eyes. One day in my late sixties, I took my grandson to the orthodontist's office and I wore a blue outfit. When the nurse came out to call him back she looked at me and said oh your eyes are blue. She called the other nurses out and said look at her eyes, they are beautiful the same color of her outfit. I was always intrigued by Newton's laws of relativity from my sociological perspective. The third law states that for every action (force) in nature, there is an equal and opposite reaction. However, his first law states that every object will remain at rest or in uniform motion in a straight line unless compelled to change its state of action of an external force. If your thinking is that there is something wrong with a blue-eyed African American woman or one cannot exist, therefore your thinking will remain at rest. We as African American women and white American women have developed our own pluralistic type of relationship which demonstrates that there is a difference between what we know is right our moral norms and what we choose which is our particular cultural norms. We look at each other from our cultural norms and declare them to be right even though we know they are wrong.

Recently, report after report of sexually inappropriate behavior has dominated the news. Prominent women have come forward accusing powerful men with sexual harassment, sexual abuse, rape and sexually inappropriate behavior. Thus, the MeToo movement took off. Women from all walks of life have found a voice because other women were courageous enough to come forward about abuses they suffered.

Where do women of color fit into this movement? Or, are women of color not victims of this abuse of power by men (or women of power)? Women of color are largely excluded from conversations around sexual misconduct by men. Accusations have been against white men by white women; however, reports of sexual misconduct by R. Kelly with women of color have gone on for years. R. Kelly is accused of underage sexual relationships, child pornography and holding against the will (kidnapping).

Lack of discussion about Kelly's misconduct may be because his accusers are not celebrities or other high-profile women. His accusers are black. Would the conversation about Kelly change if his accusers were white women? This brings us to the question, "are black women and girls viewed as worthy of attention and protection"?

Lupita Nyong, in a New York Times article, spoke out about her encounters with Harvey Weinstein. According to Nyong, Weinstein propositioned Nyong. When she emphatically declined his proposition, he told her she would never have a career. "It is her account that Weinstein and his team pushed back on." We are not only excluded from the narrative, when women of color do speak up, we are lying.

Ironically, the MeToo Movement was started by Tarana Burke, a black woman, 10 years ago, to connect underprivileged victims of sexual harassment and abuse. She did not start the movement for affluent white women but for all racial and socio-economic strata. An issue brought to the forefront by a black woman is eclipsed by white women. The white women have more resources available to deal with any issue presented to them including sexual misconduct scenarios.

The CDC reports women of color experience higher rates of sexual violence. The United States Bureau of Justice reports low-income women experience higher rates of sexual violence. The Equal Employment Opportunity Commission (EEOC) received 85,000 sexual harassment complaints between 2005 and 2015. Complaints came from the service industries, retail and manufacturing, yet white affluent women became the face of the MeToo Movement. Blue collar and minority communities are left out of the conversation. Gabrielle Union told the New York Times it is "not a coincidence whose pain is taken seriously." White women's concerns are elevated in every arena life. It is as though women of color do not exist or more accurately, do not matter.

CONCLUSION

**In the last resort, a man rightly prefers his
own interest to that of his neighbors.
-Oliver Wendell Holmes**

Racial injustice still cruelly endures. Despite the work over generations of community leaders, religious figures, public servants and average Americans, racial discrimination and hatred remains entrenched in our society whether consciously or unconsciously. There is no ship coming to take us away to another land. We are not going anywhere. If we choose not to build meaningful relationships, our power in the combination of our individual skills and knowledge will be lost.

Admittedly we all have biases and it is important that we recognize them and deal with them. This book is about the core of black and white women's real relationships. Looking at a picture over and over and long enough you may see a different image. Whether you like the image or don't like the image, African American women and white American women will still be here if you choose to look again. Every inch of the black woman has been used without compensation. What about you?

And if you harm us, shall we not revenge? (Shakespeare)

WHAT NEEDS TO BE SAID

1. How dare you think we would vote for Sarah Palin because she is a female and Donald Trump who gropes women?
2. We are not stupid, there is a price for everything. What have you paid?
3. Why is your child on the little yellow bus?
4. We don't want to say hello to your dogs. Don't you get it; dogs don't talk?
5. Your daughter will not be a rock star. Have you heard her sing?
6. Little Jackson is not precocious; he is dumb.
7. Don't tell us how smart your husband is. We went to school with him.
8. There is no hair left on your legs. You can quit shaving.
9. Yes, this my natural hair. No, you cannot touch it.
10. I don't live in the ghetto, do you?
11. No, my son does not play ball. Why are you asking me?
12. Yes, I went to college.
13. I have traveled abroad so quit pretending you have.
14. Mac and cheese is not a dinner.

15. You don't have a summer home in Florida. You have a trailer in a trailer park.

16. Don't invite me to breakfast or lunch if you don't want to eat.

17. Let your children walk to school. Do not ride them on the golf cart. They are fat.

WHAT AFRICAN AMERICAN WOMEN WANT WHITE AMERICAN WOMEN TO KNOW

www.RoyaltyFreeLogo.co

1. It is an insult to think we will vote for a person just because she is a female. Remember Sarah Palin?

2. Women have babies every second, every minute, every hour of the day. We dropped babies in the fields as slaves and then worked until the sun went down. We don't need to know details about yours.

3. It takes more than a big butt to be a black woman. The first qualification is to be born one.

4. White women that only like black men with money don't you get it? You owe us for slavery. We don't owe you. It is your turn to work, we are exhausted.

5. Quit calling what you are doing dancing like black women. There is more to it like keeping time with the music.

6. Hair slingers: We know you have hair. We don't need to have you holding your head down and standing up to get a good sling in our face. Enough with the slinging, flipping, twisting, pulling; get out of our face!

7. If you need a message get one at the spa. We are tired of seeing your husband messaging your back in church and other public places.

8. Speaking of church; buy some church clothes. There is a difference you know.

9. Don't invite us out to lunch if you are not going to eat. We don't want to share a fourth of a sandwich with you or half of our dessert.

10. Plastic surgery is not your best friend. Get a life; keep the body that God gave you.

11. Cooking and cleaning is hard work and not fun. If you don't think so follow us back from slavery to mammies, to modern day maids.

12. You don't know us so take your opinion and get off tv.

13. There are other things to do besides tennis and golf. We know how to play also. You don't own tennis and golf anymore.

14. Yes some of our friends are white. We don't care if you have black friends; we do too.

15. Life is not fair. You are privileged. Admit it.

16. All your daughters are not pretty. Some are fat and ugly; therefore, they don't need to be in a cheerleader or dance outfit.

17. We don't want your white husband, just their money to pay for what their forefathers got for free.

18. We are tired of you complaining that you can't find a good cleaning lady. Not having a cleaning lady is not a hardship.

19. Thank God for black TV channels. We are so tired of seeing you.

20. There are some black men that don't want you or want to grab your purse so get on the elevator.

21. You are not all smart, we went to school with you. Your husbands are not all smart either. We also went to school with them.

22. We remember when all your butts were flat.

23. Getting a nose job does not make you look better. A nose job just makes you feel better; save your money.

24. Mac and cheese for dinner? Your kids are hungry. Get some food stamps.

25. A half of a grilled cheese is not a meal eat the whole sandwich.

26. Our kids can play Lacrosse they just don't want to. You can't escape us. Quit trying.

27. We can't all sing, and we can't all dance. Surprise!

28. There is a black history month; observe it. You may be black and don't know it.

29. Some pants need a butt.

30. Hot dogs and hamburgers are not the only things that can be grilled.

31. Train your kids at home and we won't need daycare at church.

32. Watch out for ghetto names before you name your child.

33. We don't want to say hello to your dog. Dogs don't talk; have some children.

34. Those are not herbs in your flower pot. They are weeds. Where did you buy them?

35. You don't have a beach house. That's the life guard tower.

36. You don't have a mountain home. Your husband is a forest ranger.

37. You don't need an extended SUV because your kids need ladders to get in and out.

38. Move to a less expensive house; you are renting anyway. Your kids are tired of tomato soup and grilled cheese.

39. Buy some maternity clothes; we are tired of looking at your belly button.

40. Barak Obama was president. Yes, he was black. The end.

41. You are not rich. No one is talking about you when they talk about tax breaks.

42. There is something wrong with people who don't want other people to have health insurance. You will die also.

43. You can't afford Starbucks. Quit putting your generic coffee in Starbucks cups.

44. If you don't quit slinging your designer purse in my face I am going to attack you.

45. You are not bored. Get up off the couch and clean your house. The maid service only comes once a month; the day before you invite your friends over.

46. Cooking was not glamorous when our moms were doing it for your family.

47. We are going to your doctor husbands because our insurance pays for it. We don't want your white husbands looking at our bodies no more than you want our doctor husbands looking at yours.

48. Go ahead to McDonalds, we don't care. We know you don't have money for Five Guys.

49. Quit calling committee meetings to form more committees. We know what we are supposed to do. Let us do it.

50. Your daughter will not be on homecoming court; neither were you.

51. Your daughter will not be on prom court; neither were you.

52. Don't touch my hair! I mean it!

53. Yes, it is my real hair! No, I don't have a weave or wig. Do you?

54. You may not be white if your ancestors were here before the Civil War, do a DNA test!

55. Every child does not need a boot brace on their leg. It is only a bruise.

56. Every child does not need braces. Didn't you learn from the boot brace?

57. Yes, we read, go to the ballet, symphony and some of us even like country western music.

58. Your daughter is not a princess; she is fat, obese, big or chubby!

59. If you can read, you can cook. If you can't read, you can't cook.

60. We don't know if you can sing. We can't hear you.

61. You are poor? Get a job.

62. We know you can have babies; now quit having them.

63. Time out is not working for your child. He needs a spanking.

64. We don't want to share our lunch with you; we are hungry.

65. Quit trying to pretend you have a maid; that is your mother-in-law.

66. Didn't you know that your property was rezoned? You are living in the hood.

67. Your child is in a day care not a country day school; there is a big difference.

68. Fast food does not count as eating out.

69. Is that the same designer purse that your mom had?

70. Your child is out of control. Seek therapy.

71. Your body does not fit all jeans.
72. Your breast are too big for the rest of your body. They make your head look small; we know you bought them.
73. If you don't understand black movies, stay home. Your frequent questions are annoying.
74. If you are jogging, jog. If you are walking, walk. There is a difference.
75. Your biracial daughter needs to go to a black hair stylist.
76. Everyone does not look good as a blonde.
77. We have family values, what are you talking about?
78. Speak up so we can hear what you are gossiping about.
79. We don't like s'mores! We don't like marshmallows and crackers together. Neither do our children. Leave us alone.
80. Put some underclothes on; we can see the crack of your butt.
81. Quit standing by your cheating husband; you look stupid.
82. What was your husband doing in the hood last night?
83. Don't touch me, don't hug me. I don't like being that close to another person.
84. We all don't go to the same church; some of us go to church with you.
85. There is no hair on your legs; quit shaving!
86. It is Target, not Tar Je'.
87. I am not bringing a casserole to your house; if you don't have food don't invite me to dinner.

88. You have major issues; get help!

89. Think outside the box. You are boring.

90. Think before you wear spandex.

91. We are tired of being smarter, faster, stronger and better.

92. That's what we said! Do you understand me?

93. Don't pretend you are not in it for the money. Money, Money, Money!

94. Our food just tastes better.

95. You shouldn't be home schooling your children. Remember, you were in the slow class.

96. We want to go home from the parents meeting. How long can you discuss teachers' gifts?

97. If at first you don't succeed you are not talking about us.

98. Some of us tan also; you don't have a patent on it.

99. Look behind you, we are not following you; we are out front.

100. This is how we do it. Accept it!

101. Your child does not need a pediatrician; he needs a psychiatrist.

102. We may not want to be your friend. We have friends.

103. Get a job. You need to keep busy. You are affecting our mental health.

104. We already have friends they just don't work with us.

105. We know who you are, we just don't understand you.

106. Always remember, we are all women.

107. Don't you just love us?

Humor

A black woman riding on a train had a white woman reach over and take a bug off her shoulder. Put it back the black woman said.

Black folks can't have anything without white folk trying to take it.

SOURCES

Modi, Chuck, Instagram, Born Black, July 11, 2017.

Malcom X, *Who Taught you to Hate Yourself?*, https://genius.com, May 5, 1962 speech.

Forward

Advertisement: TV One, Sister Circle, 2018.

Chapter One

Tahir, Shah, in Arabian Nights: A Caravan of Moroccan Dreams, https://www.goodreads.com/quotes.

Albee, George, Canetto, Silvia, Sefa-dedeh, Araba (Landrine), *The Intersection of Race, Class and Gender on Diagnosis*, https://psycnet.apa.org, April 1991.

Chen, Rosalie, Newt Gringrich: *White's Don't Understand Being Black in America*, Time.com, July 8, 2016.

Jacobs, Harriet A., *Incidents in the Life of a Slave Girl, Seven Years Concealed*, edited by child, Lydia Maria Francis, 1802-1880 ed., Thayer and Eldridge, 1861.

Women in Slavery, https://oldweb.sbc.edu/sites/Honors/Women in Slavery.docx.

Fox-Genovese, Elizabeth, *Within the Plantation Household; Black and White Women of the Old South*, The University of North Carolina Press, December 1988.

Wilder, Craig Steven, *Ebony & Ivy: Race, Slavery and the Troubled History of American Universities*, Bloomsbury Press, First Edition, September 17, 2013.

Zarle, William, *Narrative of the Life of Fredrick Douglass*, Anti-Slavery Office, May 1, 1845.

Madame LaLaurie, *The Sadistic Slave Owner of the French Quarter*, www.historicmysteries.com, February 28, 2017.

Mirza, Aisha, *White Women Drive Me Crazy*. www.buzzfeednews.com, May 23, 2017.

Chapter Two

Bean, Robert Bennett, Some Peculiarities of the Negro Brains, American Journal of Anatomy, first published 1906.

Kenny, Tanasia, *Woman at Center of Emmet Till Murder Case Admits She Lied at Trial of His Killers*, https://the guardian.com-us-news, January 27, 2017.

White, Deborah Gray, *Females in the Plantation South*. NY: W.W. Norton. From Thavolia Glymph, *Out of the House of Bondage in Between the World and Me*. Ta-Nehisi Coates, Spiegel and Graw, NY.

Chapter Three

Buddha, www.quotes.net/quote/3524.

Teacher Fired Over Racist Comments About Michelle Obama, https://theGrio.com, October 3, 2016.

Hope, Clover, *Michelle Obama says Racism she Faced as First Lady 'Cut me the Deepest'*, https://Jezebel.com, July 26, 2017.

Shetterly, Margot Lee, *Hidden Figures*, William Marrow and Company, September 6, 2016.

Chapter Four

Raybon, Patricia, From Bitter Root to Flower of Forgiveness, Wings of Grace Readings, September 3, 2017.

Johnson, R. U., *Dictionary of Quotes*, https://books.google.com.

Sandler, Lauren, *White Women Need to Check Their Privilege After the Women's March*, www.timeincnet.com, January 25, 2017.

Williams, Sherri, *Historic Exclusion from Feminist Spaces Leaves Black Women Skeptical of March*, www.nbcnews.com, January 21, 2017.

Anderson, L. V., *White Women Sold Out the Sisterhood and the World by Voting for Trump*, www.slate.com/humaninterest, November 9, 2016.

Greenberg, Jon, *10 Examples that Prove White Privilege Protects White People in Every Aspect Imaginable*, https://everydayfeminism.com, November 26, 2015.

Patten, Tim, *White Female Privilege and the Domination of men*, https://ncfm.org, December 14, 2015.

Stanton, Elizabeth Cady, Anthony, Susan B., Gage, Matilda Joslyn, and Harper, Ida Husted, *The History of Women's Suffrage*, Susan B. Anthony and Charles Mann Press, 1881.

Zelonka, Caroline, Kes Sparhawk Amesley, *"Do White Female Americans Realize Their Privilege*, www.quora.com, Updated September 1, 2016.

African American Policy Forum, *Say Her Name Report*, www.aapfsayhernamereport.com, July 16, 2015.

Persons Shot by Police Database, https://WashingtonPost.com/graphics/policeshootings.

Chapter 5

Zora Neale Hurston, "Sometimes, I feel discriminated against, but it does not make me angry. It merely astonishes me. How can any deny themselves the pleasure of my company? It's beyond me.", https://brainyquote.com/ZoraNealeHurston.

Diversity, https://www.merriam-webster.com/dictionary/diversity.

Diversity, www.Gladstone.uoregion.edu/asuomca/diversityinit/definition.html.

Kendall, Francis E., PhD, *Understanding White Privilege*, from Harry Brod, *Work Clothes and Leisure Suits: The Class Basis and Bias of the Men's Movement*, in Men's Lives ed. Michael S. Kimmel and Michael Messner, NY, MacMillen 1989.

Bramen, Lisa, *The Genetics of Taste*, https://Smithsonian.com, The Smithsonian Magazine, May 21, 2010.

Address Before Democratic National Convention, https://www.pbs.org.wgbh/pages/frontline/jessie/speeches/jesse84speechhtml, July 18, 1984.

The Coretta Scott Letter on Immigration, https://TheDailyCaller.com, February 9, 2017.

Garcia-Navarro, Lulu, *When Black Women's Stories of Sexual Abuse are Excluded from the National Narrative*, Interview with Karen Attiah on NPR, December 3, 2017.

Chapter 6

Lowell, J.R., The Vision of Sir Launfal, II, https://d.lib.rochester.edu/camelot/text/lowell, 1848.

Chapter 7

Fosdick, Harry Emerson, Harry Emerson Fosdick Quotes About Hate, The Wage of Hate, www.azquotes.com.

Grundset, Eric, National Daughters of the American Revoltion, https://blog.dar.org.eric-g-grundset-director-dar-library.

Maslin Nir, Sarah, *For Daughters of the American Revolution, A New Chapter*, https://nytimes.com/for-daughters-of-the-american-revolution-more-black-members, July 3, 2012.

https://history.org/history/teaching/slavelaw.cfm, *Slavery and the Law in Virginia: Colonial Williamsburg Official."*

Heathcote, Charles William Ph.D, *Franklin's Contributions to the American Revolution*, Excerpted from a summary of an address delivered in the Washington Memorial Chapel on February 22, 1956, https://www.ushistory.org/valley/forge.

Chapter 8

Bethune, Mary McLeod, https://fancyquotes.com/Mary-McLeod-Bethune.

Finley, Taryn, *Black Girls are Viewed as Less Innocent Than White Girls Starting at age 5; Study*, https://huffingtonpost/you/black/girls, June 7, 2017.

Epstein, Rebecca, Black, Jamilia, Gonzalez, Thalia, *Girlhood Interrupted: The Erasure of Black Girls' Childhood*, https://www.law.georgetown.edu/poverty-inequality, June 27, 2017.

Goff, Phillip, Jackson, Matthew C., *The Essence of Innocence: Consequences of Dehumanizing Black Children*, https://www.apa.org/pubs/journal, February 24, 2014.

Truth, Sojourner, *Ain't I a Woman too*, Anti-Slavery Bugle, Salem, Ohio, June 21, 1851.

McGrath, Rachel, *Nicki Minaj Slams Kanye West for Rapping That Rich Black men Want to* be *with White Women*, https://www.dailymail.co.uk, October 15, 2016.

Chapter 9

Davis, Bridgett M., The World According to Fannie Davis, Little, Brown and Company, Hatchette Book Group, January 2019.

Chapter 10

www.goodreads.com/quotes/quotablequotes/BangambikiHabyarimana.

Hanbury, Mary, *Furious Walmart Customers Post Videos of Stores Locking up African American Beauty Products*," https://www.businessinsider.com/walmart-locking-up, January 26, 2018.

Moore, Maya, *Maya Moore, A Pioneering Spirit*, www.mayamoore.com/2018/01, January 29, 2018.

Wang, Amy B., *Harvey Weinstein, accused by dozens, specifically disputes Lupita Nyongo's harassment claims*, https://www.washingtonpost.com/news, October 21, 2017.

Kirschner, Hayley, *We're Going to Need More Gabrielle Union*, https://nytimes.com/2017/12/05/style, December 5, 2017.

Holmes: A Legend in Search of Demystification," Reviewed by Harvard Law Review, Vol 103, No. 3, https://jstor.org/stable, January 1990

Shakespeare, William, *The Merchant of Venice*, Act III, Scene I, https://www.goodreads.com/quotes.

Coauthor
Brenda Y. Person Ph.D.
BA Degree Youngstown State University
MA Degree Slippery Rock State University
Ph.D. Former Orlando University (Barry University)
Advance Studies: University of Cincinnati, Rollins College

Credits: Second Time Around, Author House
Ancestry: African, European, Asian, Native American

Brenda and grandson, Gregory
Paris, France

Brenda and Jane
London, England

Brenda

Coauthor
Jane K. Fieldings
BGS Degree Youngstown State University
Paralegal Certificate Kennesaw State University
Additional Studies:
     University of Georgia
     Oglethorpe University

Ancestry: African, Western European

Brenda Y. Person Ph.D.

Brenda resides in Winter Garden, FL with her husband, Gregory and son Jibri.

ashaperson@yahoo.com

Jane K. Fieldings BGS

Jane resides in Marietta, GA.

Jkf753@gmail.com

Printed in the United States
By Bookmasters